The Hock-tide observance at Hexton in Hertfordshire; together with some suggestions regarding its origin and significance

Gerish, William Blyth

BIBLIOLIFE

The Hock-tide Observance at Hexton in Hertfordshire;

together with some suggestions
regarding its origin and significance

By

W. B. Gerish

Bishop's Stortford

1910

HOCK-TIDE AT HEXTON;

TOGETHER WITH SOME SUGGESTIONS REGARDING ITS ORIGIN AND SIGNIFICANCE.

By W. B. Gerish.

OUR Hertfordshire customs are so few and so rapidly passing out of knowledge that it seems desirable, as the opportunity occurs, to place them upon permanent record   The observance of Hock-tide was one of these which (although probably in the Early and Middle Ages prevalent throughout Hertfordshire and other counties) has long been discontinued. Even at Hexton, when Francis Taverner set down his account of the festival nearly three hundred years ago, it was, one would judge, more in the nature of a recollection than a survival. He says :

I am conceited that in this place the Danish yoke lay heavy upon them (the inhabitants), for I have not heard in any place in this kingdom that Hoc Monday, or the feast of Hoc-tide or Hux-tide, which signifies a tyme of skorne and contempt, which fell upon the Danes by the death of Hardi-canute, their king, by whose death the English were freed from the Danish yoke. I say, that in the memorie of some yet lyving, this Hoc-tide feast was yearly solemnized by the best inhabitants, both men and women, in Hexton, in the fields and streetes, with strange kind of pastime and jollities. Some of their sports, and, namely, that of pulling at the pole, I will relate.

They did yearly, against everie Hock Day, elect two officers called the Hockers, a man and a woman, whose office it was to provide the hock ale, and to gouern and order the feast for that year ; these hockers had each of them a large birchenn broome , and on Hock Monday morning which falls out, as I take it, between Easter and Whitsontyde, many, and amongst them the most substantiale of them (for boyes and girles were not admitted) did go together to the toppe of Weyting Hill ; on the very toppe of which hill, being the highest in this parish, was one of those borowes or grave hills (which now the mattock and the plow have worne downe) And ther was yearlie a long and a very strong ashen pole fastened into the ground, which the women with great courage did assale and pull downe, striving with all their force to bring it downe the hill, which the men did defend pulling it up the hyll ; but by reason of the great stepenes of the mountayne, the women, by that advantage, hayled it to the fote of the hill ; and, though the men were so waggishe

I

HOCK-TIDE OBSERVANCE

as that when they perceived the women to pull most stronglye, then, they would all wholy lett goe, wherby the women fell over and over ; yet for that the women would not give over, and, when they had brought ye pole to levell ground, then some good fellowes would helpe the women, the hockers laying lustilye about them with their bromes, and allwayes the matter was so handled that the women overcame, thrusting the men into the ditches and into the brooks (the men hockers allwayes taking the womens parte) , and if they got any of the weaker men into their hands whom they could master, them they would baffle and besmear, and thus they laboured incessantlye two or three houres, not giving over till they had brought the pole and sett it up at the Crosse by the Towne House doore, where a great number of people were attending their coming. And then, the women having provided good cheere, they brought it into the Towne House, and did there all eate and drink together, and that without any affront or dislike taken at any hand. And, after they had eaten, then the hockers did gather money of everie one what they pleased to give, part of it then given to the poore, the remaining money the hockers delivered unto the churchwardens, who lay'd out the same in the reparation of the Church and bells, and the like I fynde, in an old book of churchwardens accounts, beginning about the 24th of King Henry the Eighth, that the hockers usually gave to the churchwardens of that tyme, which was collected in this manner, about 20 s. sometymes more and sometimes lesse.

Now in the after noone, they went all into the play close, where, amongst other sports, the women ran all on one side at base against the men ; and if they toke any of the weaker men prisoners they would use them unhapilye inoughe. I thinck these nicer tymes of ours would not only despise these sports, but also account them ymodest, if not prophane. But those playne and well meaning people did solace themselves in this manner, and that without offence or scandall.

I have the rather revyved the memory of this sport of pulling at the pole, because, in my understanding, it doth lyvely represent unto us the deliverance from the Danes In their assaylling of the fort, and that, chiefly by the women for their hate to the Lurdanes, their beating them with poles, with besomes, then kicking them into the kennells and bemyring their faces, and that with all maner of hockerie and scorne unto them. After all which they ate and dranck and gave money to the poore

And these solemnityes of hocking contynued for some few yeares within the reigne of Queene Elizabeth, and soe likewise did their maying feasts, with their playes of Robyn Hood and Little John

Some brief notes upon the custom may be of interest. First, the origin of the term *Hock* This has proved a crux to

HOCK-TIDE OBSERVANCE.

philologists: even that great work "The Historical English Dictionary" gives it up as hopeless. Whether *Hock* and *Hook* may not be synonymous, and *Hock* refer to the rope or chain having a hook* by which the victims were captured, is a debatable question. On the other hand, the word may have been used metaphorically, typifying that the Danes were rendered powerless as a horse that is hocked, *i.e.*, the hind sinews cut.

The authorities in question (the editors of the H E D.) reject the suggestion that it means high (a high or good time), or mockery and derision (referring perhaps to the rough, uncouth behaviour of the participants in the game), so thus the problem is left unsettled.

The next point is, what event, if any, does the observance celebrate ? The most popular belief was, that it commemorated the massacre of the Danes on November 13th, 1002, at the instigation of Æthelred the Unready. The first to record this incident seems to have been Henry of Huntingdon in his "History of England to the time of Stephen" (circa 1150). Simeon of Durham in his "History of the Kings of England from 616 to 1130," and Alured of Rievaulx, in his "Chronicle" describing Stephen's Battle of the Standard, both mention the massacre, as also do Ralph de Diceto, the Saxon Chronicle, Florence of Worcester's Chronicle, Peter Langtoft's Chronicle of England, and Robert of Gloucester's History, but all these writers make no allusion to the Hock-tide celebration of the event.

Of the other chroniclers of the period, Higden in his "Polychronicon," says the event happened on St. Brice's Night. Fabyan states in his "Concordance of Historyes," that it occurred on St. Brice's Day, 1012 , he adds, that the place where it began is uncertain, some saying at Welwyn, Hertfordshire, others at Howahil, Staffordshire. Grafton, in his "Chronicle," follows him in the same words. Holingshed's "Chronicle" makes it to have taken place on St. Brice's Day, 1012. Matthew of Westminster in his "Flores Historiarum," gives more particulars of the slaughter than any other historian, and dates it 1012, but says nothing of Hock-tide in this connection. Stowe in his "Annales or a General Chronicle of England," mentions the event as having occurred on St. Brice's Day, 1002.†

* The Staff, having a hook for reaching down carcases, used by butchers, is called a hock.

† Dugdale, in his "History of Warwickshire," 1656, p. 166, speaking of the sports at Kenilworth Castle in 1575, before Queen Elizabeth, says: "Hither came the Coventry men and acted the ancient play, long since used in that City, called ' Hock's Tuesday,' setting forth the destruction of the Danes in King Ethelred's time ''

HOCK-TIDE OBSERVANCE

The story of the massacre and its consequences is vividly depicted by Green in his "History of the English People" (vol. I, pp. 116–117). He says.

A sudden panic betrayed him (Æthelred) into an act of basest treachery which ruined his plans of defence at home. Urged by secret orders from the King, the West Saxons rose on St Brice's Day and pitilessly massacred the Danes scattered among them Gunhild, the sister of their King Sweyn, a Christian convert, and one of the hostages for the peace, saw husband and child butchered before her eyes ere she fell threatening vengeance on her murderers Sweyn swore at the news to wrest England from Æthelred For four years he marched through the length and breadth of southern and eastern England "lighting his war-beacons as he went" in blazing homestead and town Then for a heavy bribe he withdrew, to prepare for a later and more terrible onset . . . In 1013 his fleet entered the Humber and called on the Danelaw to rise in his aid Northumbria, East Anglia, the Five Boroughs, all England north of Watling Street, submitted to him at Gainsborough Æthelred shrank into a King of Wessex, and of a Wessex helpless before the foe Resistance was impossible The war was terrible but short Everywhere the country was pitilessly harried, churches plundered, men slaughtered But with the one exception of London, there was no attempt at defence. . . Even London at last gave way, and Æthelred fled over sea to a refuge in Normandy With the flight of the King ended the long struggle of Wessex for supremacy over Britain.

From the difference in the date of the massacre, which took place on November 13th, and its supposed commemoration in March or April—apart from the fact that the event did not by any means free the Saxons, save temporarily, from the Danish yoke—it is difficult to comprehend how its celebration became connected with the Hock-tide festival

The explanation given by Taverner is more reasonable, namely, that it celebrated the deliverance of the country from the wanton insults and harsh exactions of the Danes, by the death of Hardicanute on June 18th, 1042

The Rev. Mr. Denne in a paper upon Hoke-day printed in "Archæologia," vol. VII , 1784, says

No similar objections can be urged to contravert the notion that the decease of Hardicanute was celebrated at the Hokeday feast, because by his death the English were for ever released from the wanton insults and boundless exactions of him and his countrymen. And, perhaps, the time and manner of keeping the Hoketyde, with other incidental circumstances may be found to warrant the appropriation of it . . . Of the manner of keeping this

4

HOCK-TIDE OBSERVANCE

celebrity no information is to be had from any of the early historians I have examined John Ross, or Rouse, who must have collected his materials for the History of Warwickshire after the middle of the fifteenth century, and he asserts what was vulgarly called Hox Tuesday, to have been a token of the deliverance of Englishmen from the servitude of the Danes by the death of Hardicanute, and writes thus of the observance of it "ludunt in villis trahendo cordas partialiter cum aliis jocis." Lambard coincides in opinion with Ross as to the origin of this festival, and adds, "that ever after the common people in joy of that deliverance have celebrated the annual day of Hardicanute's death (as the Romanes did their feast of *fugalia* or chasing out the kings) with open pastime in the streets, calling it even till this our time Hoctyde . . . But to whatever cause the death of Hardicanute may be attributed, it unquestionably occasioned a revolution so very fortunate for England, as to afford a competent reason for instituting, by general consent, a yearly joyful commemoration of it. And I am inclined to imagine, that the long tradition of the Hokeday's having a reference to a deliverance from the Danes whose domination was considered as an Egyptian bondage . . . furnish a presumptive proof of its origin."

Of Hardicanute, Green ("History of the English People," vol. i, pp 127–128) says

The love which Canute's justice had won turned to hatred before the lawlessness of his successors The long peace sickened men of this fresh outburst of bloodshed and violence. "Never was a bloodier deed done in the land since the Danes came," ran the popular song. . . Hardicanute, more savage even than his brother Harold, dug up his body and flung it into the marsh. . . . His death was no less brutal than his life ; "he died as he stood at his drink in the house of Osgod Clapa at Lambeth "

Here the same difficulty presents itself, for the dates do not agree . but it may have been deemed desirable to substitute the first two days of the week after Easter, as this was a time when work generally was suspended, and in order to interfere less with agricultural operations than if it were kept later in the year.

The account given by Nathaniel Salmon in his "Survey of England," 1731 (vol. ii, pp 414–416), is interesting, as it differs considerably from that given under Hexton in his History of Hertfordshire published three years before He says .

From Verulam, I go through Luton, in Bedfordshire, to Ravensborough Castle above Hexton, in this county, twelve miles, as saith the Itinerary This I take to be the Durocobrivœ of Antoninus. . . . The Danes had been beaten hereabouts the year after they had been successful

5

HOCK-TIDE OBSERVANCE.

at Hokenorton, in Oxfordshire. The account of this defeat we have from Matthew Florilegus, from the Archdeacon of Huntingdon and from the Saxon Annals. There is amongst them a difference of about five years, but that is tolerably exact for writers of that age. The first writes under the year 914. " Eodem anno facta est Danorum strages maxima in finibus Luitoniœ et provinciœ Hertfordiensis."

The second author hath, under the year 911, " Et post-quam redierunt domum (Dani) statim exiit alia Caterva et ivit ad Ligetune."

After discussing whether Ligetune is represented by Leighton Buzzard or Luton and giving preference to the latter place, he continues ·

This Ravensborough is called a Castle, as is many a camp in England. Dr. Stukeley brings the name from Romans-Borough ; to confirm which there is another Fortress in Northamptonshire of the same name.

The Dean of York upon Durocobrivœ makes it to signify Aquarum Concursus Dour doubtless in British signifies water. Here are two remarkable waters, one is just below the Camp at Hexton, where is such an extraordinary Flux from one spring head, as would drive a mill within a few yards. In Saxon times this was dedicated to St. Faith The other in its neighbourhood is called Roaring Meg, from the hideous noise the fall of water after rain makes from Pexon Barn, and the steep hills thereabouts.

The Camp consists of about sixteen acres single ditched, of an oval form, prodigiously fortified by Nature, accessible but at one point where the ascent is not difficult. Hence lies a road to Sandy, in Bedfordshire, the Magiovinium, I presume, of the Romans Hexton, the Parish in which Ravensborough stands, was usually written by the Saxons Heckstanestune. In the record of Domesday 'tis Hega-staneston. This of Heckstanestune by alteration of one vowel, would be Hockstanestune*. Hock or Hoke hath relation to the Danes, and thence probably Hokenorton, in Oxfoidshire, already named Hoke or Hock is a word expressing joy. Hocks-Tuesday is the day in which the Danes are said to have been massacred throughout England. Hockey Cake is that which is distributed to the people at harvest home. The Hockey Cart is that which brings the last corn and the children rejoicing with boughs in their hands, with which the horses are also attired.

In a Church Waiden's Rate of Bishop Stortford in this county, are two or three articles explaining the word into Rejoycing. This rate is for 22 of Edward IV. and for four years of Henry VII. :

* This derivation finds no favour with Professor Skeat (" Place Names of Hertfordshire," 1904, p. 47), who states that it means " Heahstan's town,'¹ literally, " the town by the high stone.'¹

6

HOCK-TIDE OBSERVANCE.

For Hokkyng Ale   ..   .   .   14s.
De exitu cujusdam Potationis vocat. Le Hok-
  kyng Ale 13s
Pro baking 6 mod. Frumenti erga le Hokkyng
  Ale   ..   ..   4d.
Memorand recept eod an pro Hokkyng Ale .. 11s 8d
El. de profic, les Greyns de ead   ..   .   8d

The history of the Fight between the Danes and Edward the Elder hereabouts, and the remarkably long Barrows [these are or were situated near the intersection of the Watling and Ikening Street, in Bedfordshire] incline me to believe the town of Hexton was originally Hockston from that remarkably victory, and probably one army had taken the camp at Ravensborough the night before it.

As far as can be traced it would seem that as early as the thirteenth century, the Monday and Tuesday after Easter were known as Hoke-days (in the Church's calendar they were called Quindena Paschœ) Hoke Tuesday was in former times an important term-day upon which rents were paid and the like. Thus Hoke Day and Michaelmas Day divided the rural year into its summer and winter halves. As early as the fourteenth century, and probably earlier, it was a popular holiday festival, signalised by the collection of money for church and parochial purposes* by roughly humorous methods and sportive customs.

It survived the Reformation, and as a festive season with traditional customs, existed in many places (notably at Hungerford) down to the nineteenth century. The common custom seems to have consisted of seizing and binding or lifting (by women on Monday, by men on Tuesday) of persons of the opposite sex, who were released upon making a small payment.† Although as a festival it had been—in common with all merrymakings—suppressed at the Reformation, it survived as a mere frolic, and recourse was had to the device of stretching ropes across the roads to stop all passers-by, who were only permitted to resume their way when they had paid a trifling tribute. The money thus obtained was spent chiefly in drink, neither the poor nor the Church obtaining any advantage therefrom.‡

* In 1406, 1409, 1410, 1414, 1416, 1418 and 1419, Proclamations were issued to the citizens of London forbidding the "Hokkyng on Hokkedayes" under penalty of fine and imprisonment In Leland's "Collectanea," 1770, p 298, will be found an inhibition of John, Bishop of Worcester, against the abuses of the Hocdays, dated April 6th, 1450 Throughout the Middle Ages, Hock-tide was recognised as a regular date or period in legal instruments.

† "Rope Monday," the Monday following the second Sunday after Easter, to which reference is made in the Maldon (Essex) Court Rolls for 1403, 1463, and 1468, evidently corresponded with Hock Monday.

‡ Mr. Glasscock, in his "Records of St. Michael's, Bishop's Stortford," gives under date 1484, "Paid for bakyng of the bredde at hokctyde, Vd.; paid for brewyng of the hokyng ale, XVId."

HOCK-TIDE OBSERVANCE.

None of the writers upon the subject, such as Brand, Hazlitt, Walsh, or others make any original attempt to explain the meaning of this forcible capture and ransom by persons of opposite sexes, nor have I gone very deeply into the matter, as at Hexton the practice does not appear to have prevailed. The custom at this place seems to have been peculiar to it, and is therefore of much greater interest from a folk-lorist's point of view, although it presents equally great difficulties when one attempts to trace its orgin and meaning The pole was clearly an emblem, but emblematical of what? Scarcely sovereignty, for if so why should the men resist the women's efforts to depose it ? Have we not here some mystical survival of pagan rites—probably of prehistoric origin ? Long before Christianity took root in this country, the advent of Spring was annually celebrated with festivals and rejoicings in honour of Ostara, the Norse Goddess of Spring. With the adoption of Christianity this festival, like many other pagan rites, instead of being forcibly suppressed, which would have proved fatal to the advance of the new religion, was wisely adapted by the Church and, still retaining the name of Easter, became the festival of the Resurrection. It is reasonable to conclude that after the religious festivities of Easter had been duly observed, the ecclesiastical authorities annually permitted the country people to celebrate the occasion in the manner to which they had been accustomed for untold generations This secular demonstration became known as Hock-tide , and its cry of Hock ! Hock ! (*Hoch* is the German equivalent for *Hail*) was the vocal expression of the joy felt for Nature's awakening, the coming of the Spring * It may also be possible to discover parallel instances of similar customs surviving at the present time among savage races. The conclusion of the struggle is, of course, a not unusual one :

> The shout of them that triumph
> The song of them that feast

echoes all through the ages, even as it does to-day.

The game of base which was afterwards played by the good folk of Hexton is of almost equally high antiquity. It survives in the " Prisoners' Base " of our schooldays. Here we have the beginnings of the village commune and the ownership of land. A family or tribe trespasses upon a tract admitted or supposed to belong to a neighbouring family or tribe, and the result is a fight and the capture by the stronger party of certain

* It is possible that the pole represents the wooden effigy of the goddess, overthrown by the women-converts to Christianity (the gentler sex being the first to be affected by emotional appeals), notwithstanding the opposition of the men The feast, too, might represent the reconciliation of Christians and Pagans.

8

HOCK-TIDE OBSERVANCE.

individuals who would be either reserved for slaves or for torture and execution   Stories of such successes or disasters would be kept alive by re-acting the incidents in the form of annual sports It was usual to hold such fairly early in the spring, before the weather became too warm for athletic games.   In the Christian era, the boisterous pastimes coming so soon after the austerities of the Lenten season, represent to some extent the natural flow of suppressed animal spirits which the approach of spring serves but to accentuate

One might venture to remark that it seems a pity that all these ancient sports have practically fallen out of use, leaving naught but cricket and football in their place   Surely it should be possible to revive many of them,† of course, where needful, substituting milder forms and gentler actions for our forefathers' admittedly boisterous frolics

W. B. GERISH.

Bishop's Stortford.

† How numerous these were, Strutt's " Sports and Pastimes of the English People " yields abundant evidence.

9

HOCK-TIDE OBSERVANCE.

ADDENDUM.

Since the above notes were written I have re-considered the suggestions there put forth respecting the origin of the festival, and I have formed the opinion that the Hock-tide epoch of jubilation and games may be but the expression of the joy that thrilled all England at the final overthrow and slaughter of the Danes at Edington in 878 * The time of the year in which this took place, a short time after Easter, coincides with the date of the observance, whereas, as I stated, the massacre of the unsuspecting Danes by Æthelred and the death of Hardicanute occurred upon widely differing dates. If this assumption is correct, it gives the key to the symbolism of the observance. The mock-battle, or trial of strength, represents the two armies, British and Danish, the former being the weaker force, less trained and worse armed—yet by courage and strategy able to capture the lofty standard with its raven banner typified by the pole at Hexton. The rough treatment of the men is emblematical of the rout and slaughter of the Danes, and the subsequent feast, the symbol of the Treaty of Wedmore which secured a lasting peace †

Ravensburgh was probably the most important Danish station in Hertfordshire, and it is reasonable to suppose sent a considerable contingent to the army which met with so signal a defeat at Edington. The evacuation of the Camp and disappearance of the oppressors, one may suppose, would continue long in the remembrance of the inhabitants, and, if the Puritan *régime* had not cut short all such rejoicings, it is possible that sounds of revelry would still be heard in this remote village on the fifteenth day after Easter Sunday.

* Blount in his edition of " Cowell's Glossary," says that Hoc Tuesday money was a duty given to the landlord, that his tenants and bondsmen might solemnise that day on which the English mastered the Danes, being the second Tuesday after Easter week.
† It may be urged against this that the Danish dominion lasted until a much later period, but it is feasible that the celebration of the final deliverance from the Danish yoke, by the death of Hardicanute, was, as a matter of ecclesiastical and agricultural convenience, timed to coincide with the earlier celebration of the Edington victory. For the peculiar form the commemoration took at Hexton, the proximity of Ravensburgh may be responsible, typifying the storming of that place by the English and the seizing of the Danish standard.

Printed by McCorquodale & Co Ltd , London

CPSIA information can be obtained
at www.ICGtesting.com
Printed in the USA
LVIC040709291111

2583LVUK00001B